Sell Any Home
Quickly For Top Dollar

by Sathish Sekar

Edition 1.0

© Copyright 2016 Sathish Sekar. All Rights Reserved.

Published using Jutoh.

Disclaimer: This content is for informational purposes only. Any real estate sales should be done with caution and full awareness of any risks. The content provided in this book was deemed accurate at the time of publication. I do not take any liability for any consequences resulting from the use of the information contained herein. You are responsible for your own choices, actions, and results.

Table of Contents

Dedication..4
Introduction...5
I. Before Market: Improvements..........................8
   HVAC..9
   Energy Efficiency...11
   Cosmetic Fixes..14
      Painting...15
      Flooring..17
      Roof...18
   Landscaping...19
   Kitchens & Bathrooms.....................................20
      Kitchen..21
      Bathrooms..23
   Basement & Attic...24
II. Before Market: Appearance............................26
   Staging...27
   Home Warranty..30
   Excess Clutter & Tidying................................31
III. On the Market: Active Listing......................33
   Agent..34
   Pricing...36
   Marketing...39
      Where Do the Best Buyers Look? (MLS)..40
      Photos...42
      Real Estate Company..................................43
      For Sale Sign..44
      Everything Else...46
   Easy to Show Home...47
IV. On the Market: Under Contract....................49

   Third Party Negotiation..................................50
      Question: Will seller take less than asking price?..53
      Question: What do we do with multiple offers?..54
      Question: How to respond to low ball offer? 56
   Ancillary Professionals...................................57
      Inspector..58
      Contractor/Handyman.................................59
      Attorney...60
      Escrow/Title Company...............................61
   While Under Contract.....................................62
Conclusion..64
Feedback..67
Sources...68

Dedication

To those hunting for fortune.

You are bold and fortune favors the bold.

Introduction

Selling your home for top dollar is not about tricks or fancy marketing. Getting top dollar means you need a proven strategy. There will be a trade off between getting top market value and the hassle of the sale. To get the most money from sale it will require more inconvenience, out of pocket expense, and adjusting your expectations.

This book will discuss how to maximize the return on your property sale. These are proven strategies to get you the most money. This book assumes you are selling a single family house. But the strategies can be applied to other residential real estate that is typically owner-occupied (e.g. condos, duplexes, multiplexes, and even townhouses).

"**Top dollar**" means the highest price a qualified buyer will pay in the open market. This top dollar price is not related to how much you paid for the property, what you want to sell for, your mortgage balance, or the cost of improvements.

The value of residential real estate is mostly comparative in nature. Residential real estate is valued compared to similar properties in the area that have sold recently. An appraiser will use the three most recent sales to establish an opinion of value. But ultimately your home is only worth what a buyer is willing to pay for it. Even if the appraised value is higher than what buyers want to pay.

Today's buyers are educated on the real estate market through the INTERNET. Nowadays they have higher expectations for move in ready homes (they see pinterest and real estate TV shows). They prefer homes they can move into without doing cleaning, repairs, or TLC. And they still want a steep discount for any sweat equity required. For as is sales, discount your property two dollars for every dollar of needed repairs.

Before your property is even on the market you can increase the sale price through...

> 1. **Improvements**. Making upgrades can increase the value of your property. But not every improvement will yield a positive return. Certain improvements bring the property up to current market standard. These are mostly cosmetic repairs.
>
> 2. **Appearance**. This makes a home show better and is emotionally appealing to buyers. E.g. Staging

Once your property is on the market, there are two phases where you can increase your results...

> 3. **Active Listing**. This deals with how your home is presented to buyers in the local real estate market. This includes hiring the right agent, pricing, marketing, and showing availability.

4. **Under Contract**. To get a buyer under contract you need third party negotiation. In the contingency period you may need some ancillary professionals to close the deal and make final arrangements before closing.

These ideas will help you find the best buyer who will pay the best price.

I hope this book has been helpful so far. Please consider leaving a book review on Amazon. Any feedback is appreciated.

I. Before Market: Improvements

These are physical improvements to the property. They are material and permanent improvements that increase your property value. Be careful as these can add up quickly. Consult with your real estate agent to see which improvements will yield the best return.

HVAC

HVAC is likely the biggest energy consumer of your home. So you should check the HVAC system for efficiency. See if the air conditioner and heater work properly. If they are really old and not fully functional, replace them. Otherwise you can get them serviced and sell the home as-is. But you may consider some green improvements as listed in the next section.

A simple maintenance item is the air filter for the furnace and central A/C unit. This is inexpensive and will improve the overall efficiency of the HVAC system. Plus it provides clean air to breathe. If the air filter is maintained, buyers will assume you have done routine maintenance on the rest of the home.

Check the A/C condenser outside. Check the fan blades for debris as you may need to power wash it. Check ducts in the attic to see if they are sealed and insulated. If air flow is obstructed, pay for a professional duct cleaning. Duct cleaning can also remove tough odors like pets, smoking, and other allergens.

For older HVAC systems, upgrade to a digital thermostat. Buyers today expect this. Programmable thermostats can set schedules for operation. This can help owners reduce energy bills. Especially if they leave their home a lot.

Generally, you should keep your existing HVAC

appliances if they are fully functional. Even if they are old, it is better to keep them if they work. You likely won't get your money back if you upgrade to a new HVAC system. This is something most buyers will not pay extra for. It is something that is assumed to be working.

Energy Efficiency

Having an energy efficient home may also increase its value. "Green" improvements tend to provide more return on investment compared to other improvements. But you are unlikely to get a dollar for dollar return. But we will discuss some of the best upgrades possible.

If you are going to replace your water heater, you can consider a tankless water heater. They heat water in a small amount and supply immediate hot water. Instead of heating many tens of gallons, you only heat up a small amount quickly. This tankless water heater is also a lot smaller.

Windows are a big expense and should be replaced only when necessary. If you have old single pane windows you can consider switching to energy efficient double pane windows. These new windows have as much aesthetic appeal as they do practical energy saving cost. Be careful as windows can get very expensive. Only replace the windows that are broken or visibly outdated. You are also better off changing the windows on the front of the house as those will improve curb appeal.

Ceiling fans are an overlooked green feature. These can help with utility bills in hot and cold weather. They help with air circulation in the summer so you can set the thermostat lower. But they can also help in winter. In reverse speed, ceiling fans recirculate the warm air down the walls to the floors.

Find ways to add more natural light. One can add a sky light or sky tube, but that may be expensive. Simpler solutions include replacing window treatments with blinds. Replace dark drapes with light drapes to let more light in. Natural lights makes a home look bigger and more inviting to buyers.

Another simple green upgrade is to upgrade light bulbs. Go from incandescent light bulbs to fluorescent/ LED ones. These bulbs may cost more, but they last longer. So the cost of ownership coupled with energy savings make them worth the investment. Nowadays you can find fluorescent/LED bulbs with a comparable light to that of incandescent lights.

Insulation in the attic can also lower energy bills. Weatherstripping around doors and windows will assist also. This can be effective in older homes.

There may be government credits for some green updates. Check for any credits in your local area. Your local utility company likely has rebates for green features such as...

- Water conserving appliances, low-flow plumbing fixtures.

- Adding solar panels, insulation, or efficient windows/doors.

- Replacing grass with native/drought-tolerant landscaping.

Be sure to highlight green features in your

marketing. These are not the most important features a buyer will look for. But it can sway their decision to buy your home and you may get a small premium on the sales price.

Cosmetic Fixes

These items are not too expensive, but they make a big difference in how your home looks. Cosmetic fixes are classified as improvements since they are permanent changes to your property.

Painting

Repainting is the most cost effective repair before selling a property. This can give great return on investment. Painting is inconvenient but makes the home look newer and more attractive.

Avoid using loud colors like yellow or lime green. Also avoid too intense colors like red or purple. You can visit model homes to see what current builders are using. Typically you want light colors. Right now gray is pretty common.

If your paint job is recent, you can do touch up paint. But it must be a true match . Check to see if you have the original paint cans, as these will have the specific color details. You may be able to get a hardware store to color match. Touch up paint should be invisible when done! If it fails, be sure to repaint.

Exterior paint also matters as it protects the property from the elements. Exterior paint that is worn can show exposed wood or cracked window frames. Some of these exterior paint issues may be lender required repairs. This paint wearing is a clear sign of deferred maintenance. If not treated, this will allow moisture to seep into the house structure. You can also try repainting stucco exteriors. Brick and stone exteriors obviously don't need paint, but may need power washing.

Earth tones are the best colors to use for exterior. You want to use conservative colors that fit in with the neighborhood. Paint colors should be simple. Usually at most a two-tone finish. Luxury homes with trim work or textured surfaces will need more guidance. Consult with your real estate agent or a decorator if in doubt.

If the painting has been deferred, buyers and their agents will question what other items have been neglected. So repainting will make your home appeal to the most buyers. Do not make a statement or be unique. The paint should be pleasant not loud.

Flooring

Flooring is more expensive, but may be needed to bring the property upto market standard.

All carpet should usually be replaced, unless it is less than a few years old. Go with a neutral color carpet. Better quality padding makes a cheap carpet feel nicer.

Generally, most rooms are preferred in hard flooring. Hard flooring means hardwood, ceramic tile, or stone. Buyers usually want hard flooring in common areas. Some bedrooms are OK to be carpeted. But typically hard surfaces last longer and are easier to clean. Remember that hard flooring is way more expensive than carpet.

Talk to your real estate agent about what flooring buyers will expect. This can get expensive so you need to be strategic and do only what is necessary to get you the best sale.

Roof

The roof is the most basic protection for any house. It protects the house from exterior elements that are falling upon it (e.g rain, snow, hail, wind). And it is usually very visible and affects a house's curb appeal. This structural component needs to be in good condition if you want to sell a house.

Roof durability depends on how expensive the shingles are. Any kind of hard roof material will last longer (e.g. clay tiles). If a roof is passable, it is better to keep it. An insurance adjustor can check if the roof is insurable. If it is, it should be good enough to sell.

If you do need to replace roof, the best solution is to put a new roof that is comparable with those of the neighboring houses. Buyers will definitely notice if it is new.

Landscaping

Landscaping helps your curb appeal. First impressions are lasting with buyers. A maintained front yard invites the buyers into the house. The landscaped backyard makes them want to stay.

Landscaping usually won't get you a good return on investment. So better to be thrifty. Focus on younger plants to make your house look younger. Flowers can also add great color. Mature trees can add charm and provide shade.

You may opt for native and low maintenance landscaping. This landscaping needs less water and is environmentally friendly. This is becoming popular in western states with recurring water shortages. This native landscaping cannot look like a weed patch. It still needs to look maintained and not overgrown/neglected.

Notice landscaping on new construction homes in the area. You can spot the trendy plants, and note the younger plants.

Kitchens & Bathrooms

Kitchens and bathrooms are the most coveted rooms in a house. They can make or break a house buying decision. Due to their heightened importance you need to make these rooms upto par. Women especially want to have nice bathrooms/kitchens. Check with a local real estate agent to see what buyers are expecting for these rooms.

These are two rooms where improvements yield a great return on investment. This does not mean dollar for dollar return though. But you are likely to get the best return in these two rooms.

As mentioned, you still need to declutter walls and countertops in kitchen and bathrooms. This step is simple and costs nothing to do other than costing inconvenience.

Kitchen

For your kitchen, remember to neatly stow away your daily appliances and possessions.

After this decluttering, you can decide if you want to make physical improvements. Consult an expert as these rooms get expensive to update. And for gods sake do not use Zillow to estimate how much value a kitchen remodel will add. Zillow wants to sell your info to a contractor, so do not rely on their estimation. Spending $10,000 on new cabinets does not lead to an extra $30,000 on your sale price. Talk to your real estate agent before upgrading and remodeling.

Kitchen appliances more than 10 years old are usually unappealing to buyers and requires replacement. Upgrading appliances can make a big difference in the look of the kitchen. Ask a real estate agent if the appliances are good enough to pass today's standards.

For fridges, consider upgrading to a stainless steel one. Also make clear to your agent if you are taking the fridge or leaving it. If you keep the existing fridge, clean it all inside and on top. Take off magnets on the outside of it.

Cabinets and countertops are also key items to examine in a kitchen. Cabinets are the most expensive of these items to replace. If they are in decent shape, it is better to refinish the cabinets and repair them. Countertops are great aesthetic boosters. Most buyers want granite today. So upgrade if they are Formica or laminate. Granite is not as expensive as people think and you can opt for a thinner granite to save costs (1.25 inches).

Light fixtures can be updated if needed. But focus on the other items in a kitchen first. Kitchen wall paper should be replaced with paint.

Bathrooms

Bathrooms get outdated quickly too.

Check if your tiles and fixtures are current. Ask your real estate agent to make the determination. Tiles tend to go out of style quickly.

You can give a bathroom a facelift by changing some small fixtures and the finishes. E.g. changing the faucets, towel bars, and holders. You can also refinish the tub to add some sparkle.

Plumbing fixtures should be changed if the bathroom is older than 10 years old. These are not that expensive and can add great value. Also look to add energy efficient, water saving fixtures. Some municipalities may require water-conserving toilets to be installed when a property sells. Also change out wall paper to regular paint. No one wants wall paper anymore.

Generally if you are changing one fixture in a bathroom. It is better off just to remodel the whole bathroom. But it depends on the cost and size of the room.

Basement & Attic

Consider what the market standard is for basements and attics. Based on this you will need to make decisions on what to improve. If there is no basement in your house then you cannot do much there. But if you have an unfinished basement you have some choices. See if other houses have finished basements and if buyers expect one. Again you should consult with a real estate agent to see what the best improvements are.

Be careful as basements can get expensive fast. You are making this improvement to help you sell the home. So you will not be enjoying the new finished basement for a long time. So you should aim to be thrifty and just do enough to entice buyers. Your best bet is to remodel basement so it is finished and livable.

If on a budget, you can just do a basic basement remodel with the framework and no room partitions. Then leave it to the buyer to finish the basement to their taste once they buy. You can just finish the outer walls and add basic flooring. Along with electrical and basic plumbing. You may be able to leave the plumbing rough in for a bathroom to be built out by the next buyer.

For unfinished basements you should still make the basement look presentable. Paint the concrete walls with concrete paint. Also use enamel paint on the floors to create a more inviting space. Move any storage in one consolidated corner, ideally in a closet.

Make sure the basement is cleaned out. Especially in the corners and ceilings. So dust out the crevices so buyers don't feel dusty or see cobwebs. Your unfinished basement should be presented as clean and look like it has potential.

The attic is another potential space for houses. Your best bet is to just clean it out and leave it for the next buyer. It is rare for finished attics to be the standard in a market.

II. Before Market: Appearance

These are strategies about changing the appearance of the property without adding to it. These are easy fixes that are relatively inexpensive.

Staging

Staging was not important until recently. Staging did not offer much benefit to homes that were clean and in maintained shape. Now because of TV and social media, buyers like to see staged houses and have higher expectations. This is especially noticeable in the higher price ranges. Lower price range buyers may not be influenced as much by staging. Also a low sale price like $100k may not justify the expense in professional staging. But those lower priced homes can still benefit from do-it-yourself staging.

A professional stager will come into your home and make it appeal to the widest cross section of potential buyers. Your house will look good to most buyers while still remaining neutral. A stager will make the house look good while still neutral.

You may have had an interior decorator do your home. You should still use staging as the decorations are tailored to you. Your decorations may not appeal to the largest cross section of buyers. Neutral decorations appeal to most buyers while alienating as few buyers as possible.

You can search online for staging ideas. So you can do some basic staging on your own, especially for a lower priced listing. Or you can ask your real estate agent to provide suggestions. Here are some basic steps to take:

- Clean the house. If needed, do a deep

cleaning to get rid of tough odors.

- Put away family photos in a box. You don't want any pictures of yourself around when buyers are looking at house. Because buyers will feel like they are intruding if they see your pictures. It is as if you are watching them.

- Put away political paraphernalia and religious symbols. These items may incite a strong response from buyers. You want the house to appeal to the widest number of buyers, not just those who think like you.

- Also put away anything that is very sensitive in nature such as decorations with sexuality or nudity. Best bet is to ask a real estate agent or stager what to put away.

When a buyer walks in, they need to feel at home. Buyers have certain requirements for their property like price, location, room count, and condition. But in the end they will pick from available properties based on their emotional judgment, not rational arguments. Buyers get emotionally attached to a property first then they rationalize their purchase. This is why non-neutral decorations will throw buyers off emotionally. You need to figure out what could stop a buyer from feeling at home in my property. Proper staging will make buyers feel at home.

Some owners may be annoyed by staging. Owners may think that if the buyer cannot see past my decorations, then too bad. But if you want to sell the house and get top dollar (remember the goal) you need to make the home show neutrally. This process is called de-personalizing the home to create maximum appeal to buyers.

You can even go look at brand new homes that have staging. Your end goal is to emulate the look of those houses. These builders know how to get buyers emotionally invested. Learn from them.

Home Warranty

A home warranty is not something that can be seen by buyers. But it still improves the appearance of your home. Buyers will think of your home as safe to buy because of the warranty. So it is a "virtual staging" upgrade.

You can increase the perceived value of your house by providing a home warranty. Most used purchases in our consumer society have some warranty. You can make your house have the same thing for a couple hundred dollars. You may end up paying for a home warranty anyway if it is standard in your market or if you are in higher price range. Mention your home warranty in your marketing as an added benefit to buyers.

Home warranty also benefits sellers during the listing period. If you start the home warranty when you are on the market, you can eliminate some "pre-existing conditions". These pre-existing conditions may prevent buyers from using the warranty if it was started at the closing of the sale. Sometimes buyers can even come back to the seller and sue for expensive repairs. A home warranty can alleviate some of this risk.

Excess Clutter & Tidying

Most people have too much stuff. Sometimes people move in order to have space for even more stuff. An over-stuffed house looks smaller and also makes it look older. It also makes the space feel unorganized and uncared for.

Excess clutter has a negative effect on buyers emotions when they see the house. Clutter creates stress. But to the owners of the house it is oblivious since they know where things are. But to potential buyers the clutter is overwhelming. It is like a maze for them to visualize themselves living there. So make it easier by getting rid of unwanted items.

Regarding the effects of tidying, read <u>the life-changing magic of tidying up</u> by Marie Kondo. This Japanese home consultant discusses how tidying will change your whole mindset and daily life. By getting rid of clutter you will feel less distracted and think clearer. Check out the book if you want to know why getting rid of clutter will improve your life physically and mentally.

How to deal with clutter. Generally speaking you have the following options: sell it, give it away, store it, or throw it away.

Go through the closets and either throw/donate clothes you don't want. Next deal with unneeded furniture. Too much furniture makes the rooms look smaller. If any furniture is not going to your next house, sell it or give it away. But for staging purposes, make sure you have enough furniture to make the house look livable.

Also focus on kitchen countertop and bathroom counter top space. The counter need to be mostly visible. The fewer items the better. This will make the kitchens and bathrooms look bigger.

Any other items you have not used in the last six months consider throwing them out. This way you can relieve yourself of the burden. Otherwise you can put them in storage.

Note that moving things from a room to the garage or closet is not getting rid of clutter. This is simply transferring the clutter to a different place in the house. Now the house feels like it has no garage or no closet space. Better off to rent storage space or throw out unneeded items.

How people live in a home is not the way they want to shop for a home. So remember that this short term inconvenience will lead to a top dollar sale.

III. On the Market: Active Listing

These are strategies to implement when your property is on the market. These include hiring an agent, pricing, marketing, and showing availability. All these strategies will help you secure the best buyer.

Agent

On top of all these strategies, you should hire a real estate agent to handle the sale for you. Using the other strategies without the guidance of a real estate agent means you are handicapping your results. Consider consulting with an agent while preparing your property for the market. An agent can advise you which projects are worth your time and money.

Look for the agent who has knowledge and skills. This is not necessarily the agent who has been selling the longest. Although years of experience may indicate this competence. Look for someone who can market your home correctly and price it so people want to buy it.

Also look for strength and honesty. Your agent needs to be strong to tell you the truth even if it not what you want to hear. This is a high dollar transaction and you need someone to tell you the honest truth about what to expect. Don't go with nice; go with competent. This agent has a fiduciary responsibility to act in your best interest. Avoid someone who only cares about getting a deal so they can get a commission.

Understand that for any other type of critical life decision, people go to a professional. For taxes, rich folks use a accountant. For estate planning, people use an attorney. For medical issues, people go to their doctors. For a real estate transaction, you need to use a real estate agent.

An agent will also help you get navigate from contract execution to a a successful closing. They will handle the transaction and the finer details. The bottom line is that a skilled agent will save you money by advising which improvements to add and which to skip. Also they will get you the best possible price. So often agent commissions are justified through their market expertise and negotiation skills.

Pro tip: Selling your home For Sale By Owner ("FSBO") is an option. But you will be dealing with a complex transaction with details that you do not handle regularly. When dealing with an asset this expensive (your home) it is better to pay for a professional to represent you. And even if you do a flat fee MLS listing. That flat fee agent is not likely to get you the best results. You need a full service agent who will handle the sale from start to finish.

Pricing

Price is the most important part of selling a property. Obviously for sellers, they aim to get the highest price. But remember the house will not sell for what you want, it will sell for a what a buyer is willing to pay for it.

To buy a house, buyers need to be excited about two things:

> 1. **Property**. The property needs great pictures online. Since most buyers will be introduced to your home through an online listing. Then once they see the property in person, they need to "feel" this is the right house. If they don't like the property, buyers will not buy it even if the price is good. If you have been following this guide so far, your property will be appealing.

> 2. **Price**. The price needs to be attractive also. And makes your home the best value out of the competition. If the price is competitive, your house will create urgency among buyers.

If your property shows well and is priced right, buyers will fight over it. You need to price it so you get the most demand and excitement. It will be like your house sale is an event. Event pricing can create urgency for buyers and urgency gets more money for sellers. These excited buyers will fall in love with the house and bring the highest offers (sometimes above asking price).

Don't try it high and come down. This approach will work against you. It will lead to more time and stress. If a house is overpriced, it sits too long on market. Then people start to wonder what's wrong with it. More time on the market leads to "staleness". Buyers want new listings, not the leftovers that other buyers passed over.

Today's buyers are well educated. They know a deal when they see it. And they also know if a house is overpriced and may not even go view it. For unreasonably priced homes, buyers are likely to ignore it completely. A high price creates the opposite of excitement. It makes buyers wary of liking the house and it is hard to get them emotionally attached.

Understand the buyers perspective. What buyers see before coming to a house is the price. And if the price is higher than the competition, they come to your home with the expectation they are not going to like it. It may be the perfect house for them and meet their requirements. but they feel like the price forces them to say no.

Being overpriced leads to slower offers and usually a lower price. A buyer may think, "Hey if the seller is 10% over, I'll start 10% under market value so we meet in middle". An unreasonably high price may also discourage buyers from submitting an offer at all.

Be wary of an agent who tells you to start high and come down. This approach will cost you equity and you will end up selling for less. And you will take longer to sell with more inconvenience. Some agents may use the approach of telling you what you want to hear. Then they get the listing overpriced and they keep bugging you for price reductions. It is better to have an honest agent tell you the truth up front and price right from beginning.

If you get an offer quickly that means you are priced where the market responds. There are a pool of buyers in your market right now looking for a house like yours. Your property listing will be seen by the buyers that are new and the ones have been looking for several months. So the best chance to get top dollar is at the beginning when the most buyers are looking at the house.

Waiting longer, doesn't result in a higher price. Buyers are most likely to buy your house in the first 2-4 weeks. After that, long market times just gets the buyer a better price. This because sellers lose their chance to get multiple offers. To get the most money, you need sell in the beginning of the listing. Do not wait for some magical buyer to come and pay over market value. It will not happen.

Remember that marketing will not increase a home's value. Marketing efforts have a limit to how effective they are. Once your home is exposed to all the qualified buyers, the job of marketing has been done. The buyers know that your home is for sale. But pricing is what will inspire buyers to want to purchase the house once they have seen it.

Marketing

In order to sell your house, buyers need to know about it. The best strategy is to generate a lot of interested buyers fast. More interest by other buyers cause people to think this is a desirable property. This leads to faster and higher offers.

To get the most interest, your home needs to be exposed to all the potential buyers in the market.

The best buyers are...

> 1. **Motivated to buy a house like yours.** They want to buy now, not later. They don't want to miss out on the right house for them.
>
> 2. **They have money** and financing to buy a house like yours.

The purpose of marketing is to get these qualified buyers looking at your house.

Where Do the Best Buyers Look? (MLS)

The best buyers find their properties on the internet and with a licensed real estate agent.

Qualified buyers will definitely use an agent since it does not cost them extra to do so. And agents have access to the most properties. Plus they get to use the agent's expertise and guidance through the process. This is better than trying to find properties on their own.

The agents that work with these buyers go to local **MLS** properties. That is, properties listed on the **Multiple Listing Service** database by other licensed agents. MLS properties have listing information that is complete and they assure that a commission will be paid if a buyer is procured. The MLS is the only place agents look for properties to show. So it is imperative your home is listed on your local MLS database.

A buyer will either see your property through MLS listings that their agent sends to them. Or they will see your listing on a public real estate website. These sites are better known by their domain names like Redfin, Trulia, Zillow, Realtor.com. They get 99% of their listings from MLS databases. So if your property is on the MLS, it is accessible to these buyers!

Pro tip: Some sellers may opt out of using an MLS listing and do a "pocket listing". A pocket listing is when the listing agent is responsible for marketing the property through personal connections only. No public marketing is allowed. Now there may legitimate personal objections to not having a public listing. You may be a celebrity or have a high net worth. So you may want to preserve your privacy and not want public marketing. But just understand you are sacrificing some critical exposure. Pocket listings are not in your best interest if you want to get top dollar. To get top dollar you need to get the most buyers looking at your home, which means you need an MLS listing.

Photos

Excellent photos on the internet get buyers interested in seeing your home. Most buyers will be introduced to your home on the internet so you need to leave them wanting more. So be sure to get professional photography and some staging beforehand to get the best photographs.

Professional photographers will make your house show well online. They can also use Photoshop to enhance any shots they take. This will create a great first impression on the internet with potential buyers. Then these buyers will want to come see your house in person.

As of late, we are seeing more advanced photography. Tools like virtual tours, drone photography, and video walkthroughs. These can help but *the most important media to have is excellent still photographs*. As most buyers will flip through pictures quickly when they see your home listed on the internet. They may not even try to look at your virtual tour or anything else fancy.

Real Estate Company

The choice of real estate company is not as important as hiring the right agent. Even a large national franchise can have bad agents working in a local office. You need to pick the right agent who is familiar with your neighborhood market and how to market your house properly. Pick the agent that will get you the best results. The right agent from a small company is better than a mediocre one from a national company. Key is to make sure the agent has the skills, knowledge, and MLS access to complete your sale.

For Sale Sign

A for sale sign is not the most important marketing tool but it can still be effective. Buyers today still drive through neighborhoods to see where they want to live. You cannot experience the "vibe" of a neighborhood on Google maps. This cannot be done on the computer. So a for sale sign alerts potential buyers that you have what they want: a house.

Some sellers are hesitant about the for sale sign. But *a product that is easier to spot is easier to buy*. The for sale sign assures buyers that your house is a potential opportunity for them. They drive up to the home and they know that this could be the "one". Don't be scared if the neighbors know you are selling. Neighbors may refer someone who wants to move into the neighborhood, like a friend or family member.

You definitely don't want bad first impressions. Like if there is no sign and the buyers can't find your house. Then they get annoyed by having to read small address numbers. Also buyers may think you're not really interested in selling if there is no sign. This is part of buyers' first impression with the property.

The last thing you want is for buyers see a house they like, but it is not the one for sale. Disappointing. They are like "Well we want that pretty house but that ugly one next door is the one on the market". Don't have buyers falling in love with the wrong house. Use the for sale sign to identify your house as the one they can buy

Maximum Exposure leads to...

Maximum Interest leads to...

the **Best Price**

Everything Else

All the other house marketing tools you hear about are useless. Only the ones previously listed matter. Due to internet technology, marketing a home is simple and automated through the MLS.

Marketing pieces like flyers, postcards, billboards, and holding open houses do not make a difference. The only reason sellers hear about these is that some agents don't know how else to differentiate themselves.

Marketing a house for sale takes a proven approach. You don't need to reinvent the wheel. You just need someone who knows how to get it done. It is like flying a plane. Do you want your pilot to try something new when they fly a plane? Or do you want them to use the process that is repeated time and time again?

Easy to Show Home

The goal is to sell the house, not make things convenient for yourself. So for a few weeks you need to make it easy for buyers to see the property. Buyers today are very busy and stressed about the big life decision of buying a house. So they need convenience and don't like weird showing restrictions. E.g. "I only show the house on 2nd Tuesdays of the month when the blue moon is out". Even in a low inventory market, buyer will skip a house if it is hard to view. Even if it is the perfect house for them otherwise. Buyers think that if the house is difficult to see, then sellers don't want to sell it to me. Buyers are irrational like this

Buying a house is chiefly an emotional decision. After location and size criteria is determined, the final selection comes down to how they "feel" about a house. Buying your house must be an easy decision to make. This starts by making it easy for buyers to see your house.

Most buyers look during the day, not evenings. Especially in higher price ranges. They can look on weekdays as well as weekends. Even the buyers at a weekend open house tend to be tire kickers, i.e. unqualified buyers who are window shopping. The motivated buyers are looking in the week trying to find the best house first.

You need to provide access on short notice to allow as many buyers as possible to look at the house.

Short notice means as little as 3-4 hours. Also allow your agent to put a lockbox. This will allow other licensed agents to show their buyers when you are not there. The lockbox allows more buyers to see your home by increasing availability. And having more buyers looking at the house will lead to a higher price.

Also when you have a showing, be sure to get the house ready. Put away miscellaneous belongings. Clear off the countertops and clean the dishes. Try to keep desks and tables organized. Also do any last minute cleaning.

Try to keep the security alarm off during showings. Turn it off before showings. Better yet only turn it on at night. If it needs to be disarmed, things can go wrong. The buyer's agent may not hit the right code. If an alarm siren goes off during a showing, buyers will be traumatized into not buying the house.

Pets should not be in a house for sale. They may be part of your family. But some buyers will not feel at home if there is pet hair. Some buyers may not even like pets. Better to have your pets stay somewhere temporary while the property is on the market. Don't have a dog growling in a cage while a buyer is trying to view your home. Cat dander can also throw buyers off. If you have had pets, you need to deep clean the house to remove the hair. You need to remove all signs of odors also. If you do choose to keep your pets in the house, you must remove them before every showing.

IV. On the Market: Under Contract

These are strategies for getting the property under contract and moving towards a closing. A property under contract means there is a sales contract signed by both seller and buyer.

- Typically this starts with negotiating an offer from a buyer.

- After contract execution, there is a contingency period to satisfy contract conditions.

- Once contingencies are removed, the sale can close and the seller moves out. At closing, the seller gets paid the proceeds from the sale.

Third Party Negotiation

Once you first communicate with a buyer or a buyer's agent, negotiations have begun. Hopefully you have taken the earlier advice of hiring a skilled real estate agent to handle your sale. Negotiations can start before an offer is even submitted. You need to be strategic in how you answer buyer questions. Motivated sellers lead to motivated offers. So as a seller, don't play hard to get. You need to communicate enthusiasm to make the deal work for both sides. Buyers want to buy the house because the deal makes them feel good emotionally. They like the price, they like the house, and they should like their perception of the seller.

If you position your home correctly, buyers will fight over the home. And you will end up getting the best price and terms. You need an agent who knows how to handle offers as they come in. Or better yet, how to handle multiple offers on your home.

An agent needs to artfully navigate questions when negotiating. Questions like "Will the seller take less?" or "Is the price negotiable?" are sensitive questions. You need an agent to answer these questions without giving away your negotiating position. But also encourage buyers to move forward.

Unfortunately, the average real estate agent does not have negotiation skills. A common mistake is to hire an agent because you are friends, they live nearby, or they are cheap. If you want the best price, this is a business decision, not a friendship decision. Hire the best agent with the skills to negotiate a very large transaction for you.

Commissions are worth the expense. Other highly paid individuals like actors and athletes, use agents to negotiate their contracts. There is skill and value in hiring a skilled professional negotiator.

A third party negotiator has advantages. First they have specialized skills and knowledge to have a stronger position. Second, they are objective and not emotionally attached to an outcome. Third, there is a communication buffer which allows for strategic responses.

Agents who don't understand negotiations can be more of a liability. Negotiating is key to getting the most money from potential offers. Negotiation skills are even more critical than a "marketing plan". Due to technology, marketing is relatively simple.

Your agent also needs to understand counter offers. You want to be firm but reasonable in counters. See if there are other terms important to the buyer besides price. Perhaps closing time or something else.

You should ask some questions to screen agents for their negotiation skills. Watch for the agent's response to these negotiating questions. If they are uncertain, then that may work against you. In these negotiating situations you need to take decisive action. Also watch for agents who become too hostile. You want a strong negotiator but not one who is a strong enemy to a buyer. Don't pick someone who wants to act like a hero. This deal must work for the seller and the buyer. A good negotiator will get the deal done faster and easier for you.

Read ahead for possible negotiation situations...

<u>Question:</u> Will seller take less than asking price?

Answer Strategy: You need an honest response that does not compromise your negotiating position, but fosters further dialogue. The agent should encourage the buyer and their agent to submit an offer and stay interested in the property.

A skilled response would be: "I'm glad to see you have an interest. Based on the similar properties that have sold, the seller feels $X is a fair price. Has your buyer seen the property?".

You need to answer the question but take control of conversation. Now you can qualify the buyer and see if there is real motivation. Or if this person just wants to low ball a property. You need an agent who sees these questions as opportunities and does not get immediately defensive. So you need someone to answer this question without giving away your price.

In this situation it can be dangerous to hire a discount agent. Think about if an agent will discount their commissions just to get listings, how easily will they discount your home price to make a sale? You need someone strong enough to negotiate their own commission as well as your home price. What is even worse is a flat fee agent who gets paid their listing commission upfront. They have no incentive to help you get the most money. Full service agents are paid a percentage of your sales price, so it is in their interest to help you sell for the best price.

Question: What do we do with multiple offers?

Answer Strategy: You need an agent with a real strategy. There are only a few ways to correctly handle multiple offers. And a million ways to screw up the situation so the seller ends up with no offers and no sale. Buyers are fickle and will tire within a few hours if their offer is not responded to. So the seller needs to respond quickly and fairly.

When you have multiple offers your options are the following: reject all offers, counter one of the offers, accept an offer, or request highest/best offer from all buyers.

Rejecting all offers is also an option. But this is stupid. You should at least see if the offers will come up through a highest/best request. Sometimes sellers will get greedy once they have multiple offers and now they want some ridiculously high price.

Countering one of the offers could work. But this is not the best choice since you don't know which of the multiple offers is willing to go the highest. Better to allow all the interested buyers to put their best offer forward.

Accepting one of the offers may be prudent if one offer is too good to wait on. And that buyer may be offended if there is a request for highest/best offer. Again this is upto the seller. The seller may be on a timeline and want to wrap this up soon. So it could be the best option for their situation.

Usually the best option is to request the highest and best offer. This will keep buyers interested and allow them to submit their best offers. Oftentimes you will get even higher prices and get more favorable terms. I.e. waiving some contingencies that allow buyers to cancel out of transactions. There is a short time span to do this highest best request so decisiveness is key.

A strong negotiator will contact all interested buyers with a message like this:

"The seller requests that all interested buyers submit their highest best offer by (date) at 5 pm.". The deadline should be within 1-2 business days. You don't want to drag this out for fear of losing impatient buyers.

A bad response is one that loses buyers. And the worst response is no response. Because you don't know what the best offer would have been.

The first round of offers while the property is on the market is almost always the best one. When a property is new it has the most buyer interest. So do not get greedy when you get multiple offers. *Understand that you have leverage but the window of opportunity is very short!*

Question: How to respond to low ball offer?

Answer Strategy: Any offer is a starting point. Always respond so you can test if the buyer is realistic. If they are still low balling, then forget them. But you never know since some buyers will start low just to see what happens and they may be willing to go much higher. And quite honestly, a low ball offer probably indicates a weak buyer's agent. So you may be able to get the upper hand in the negotiation.

Do not take a low ball offer personally. It is about your house, not you. And if a buyer can't come up in price you don't sell the house to them. Simple.

Ancillary Professionals

Once you agree to terms with a buyer and you sign the sales contract, the contingency period begins. This is the period where the conditions in the contract need to be satisfied. Once the contingencies are removed or satisfied a closing can take place.

In this contingency period you will be dealing with other related professionals.

Inspector

The buyer usually hires a home inspector soon after signing the sales contract. But the seller will need to cooperate and allow the inspector to inspect the property.

This inspector will find everything wrong with the property no matter how insignificant. When the inspectors points out issues, don't take it personally.

The seller should leave the house when the inspection is happening. If you are there you will slow down the process. Also you will get aggravated when the inspector keeps pointing out things that are wrong. So better to just leave and let the process go unhindered.

Same advice goes for other inspections like termite or municipal.

Contractor/Handyman

To close your sale you may need the services of a good contractor or handy man. Likely you will have somebody you were using for the pre-market repairs. The buyer or the buyer's lender may require certain repairs to go through with the sale. You can either choose to do these repairs, deny the repairs, or offer a repair credit.

I would highly advise giving a repair credit as opposed to actually doing repairs. If you agree to perform repairs, you are spending money anyway. And you need to manage the project to make sure the repairs get done. Plus the buyer still may not be satisfied with the way the repairs are done. So better off to just give money directly to the buyer as a closing credit. A lot of buyers will shut up and accept a repair credit if it means money in their pocket.

And usually their home inspector will be exaggerating any issues. Then once buyers move in they never do the repairs cause they are insignificant.

Attorney

Depending on your state, you may want an attorney to review the sales contract. Talk to your real estate agent and see what the standard practice is. The attorney would review the contract to make sure it is aligned with what you expect. The attorney may also make the formal revisions to the contract after execution. They can request extensions, negotiate repairs, etc.. They may also represent you as the seller at the closing.

Your real estate agent cannot technically give legal advice. So seek advice from an attorney if needed.

Escrow/Title Company

Depending on your state, your closing will take place at either an escrow or title company. This is the entity that handles the money involved in the transaction. And when the transaction is consummated the money will be disbursed according to the contract. Basically this company will pay you, the seller, the money from the sale.

Sellers do not usually pick the closing company. As they usually go with the closing company that their agent or attorney suggests. Oftentimes the real estate agent may have a closing company that they use in their office. Again you still have the right to pick your closing company. But it is best to go with the one recommended to you since it will make for a smoother transaction. Check if the closing company is legitimate. Any legitimate closing company can easily furnish their license and insurance information.

While Under Contract

While under contract, do not change anything about the property. Buyers signed the contract when they saw the property in its current state. And the property needs to stay in that state to avoid contract default. Don't do anything drastic like repainting. Maintain status quo.

Remember you are still owner of the property until you close the transaction. As such, you are responsible for general maintenance and paying any related bills. Any deferred maintenance may cause further delays. Keep paying the mortgage and the taxes. Also keep paying utility bills and keep utilities on for any inspections.

Start planning your next move. Look for your next home if needed. Get estimates from moving companies. I would suggest waiting until closing date is scheduled before fully ordering from a moving company.

Be sure to clean the house after moving out. You can also consider a professional cleaner if you need to get rid of odors or allergens. Most real estate contracts require the house to be in broom swept condition when the seller moves out.

When you move out, be sure to leave behind your house keys. Also don't forget your garage opener remote. A lot of people forget this in their cars.

Conclusion

This information, when applied, will maximize the return on your property sale. First you make your property as desirable as possible through its appearance and improvements. Then you need to market and price it correctly. On top of it all you need the right agent to guide you in this process.

Currently, I work as a real estate agent. So a lot of these strategies are from my experience and from my real estate training. I would like to thank my fellow colleagues and the coaches/mentors who have imparted their information.

I have also written another book on flipping houses. This book covers how to pick a house to fix and flip it as an investment. Search on Amazon for Pick Your Flip: 100+ Picture Guide To Flipping Houses.

I hope this book has been helpful. Please consider leaving a book review on Amazon. Any feedback is appreciated (positive or negative). Feel free to email comments to me, sathish306@gmail.com

Best of luck,

Sathish Sekar

Real Estate Agent/Investor

Feedback

I welcome any feedback for this book. As mentioned in the conclusion, please leave a review if you enjoyed this book. The reviews will help my book gain credibility and exposure. Feel free to be honest in your reviews. All negative and positive feedback is greatly appreciated.

<u>Please leave a book review on Amazon</u>, or email me at sathish306@gmail.com.

Thank you again,

Sathish Sekar

Sources

TOP-DOLLAR: The 10 Proven Strategies to Make Your House Sell Faster and For More Money. by Kevin Ward.

the life-changing magic of tidying up: the Japanese art of decluttering and organizing. by Marie Kondo.

Flipping Houses for Dummies. by Ralph Roberts with Joe Kraynak.

www.ingramcontent.com/pod-product-compliance
Lightning Source LLC
Chambersburg PA
CBHW021414170526
45164CB00002B/641